The Anointing of Faith-Based Affirmations

The Anointing of Faith-Based Affirmations

A Parental Guide to Help Children Using
The Word Of God

FLORINE G. FREEMAN

XULON PRESS

Xulon Press
555 Winderley Pl, Suite 225
Maitland, FL 32751
407.339.4217
www.xulonpress.com

© 2024 by Florine G. Freeman

Contribution by Carol Myrthil-Dickerson

All rights reserved solely by the author. The author guarantees all contents are original and do not infringe upon the legal rights of any other person or work. No part of this book may be reproduced in any form without the permission of the author.

Due to the changing nature of the Internet, if there are any web addresses, links, or URLs included in this manuscript, these may have been altered and may no longer be accessible. The views and opinions shared in this book belong solely to the author and do not necessarily reflect those of the publisher. The publisher therefore disclaims responsibility for the views or opinions expressed within the work.

Unless otherwise indicated, Scripture quotations taken from the Amplified Bible (AMP). Copyright © 1954, 1958, 1962, 1964, 1965, 1987 by The Lockman Foundation. Used by permission. All rights reserved.

Scripture quotations taken from the New King James Version (NKJV). Copyright © 1982 by Thomas Nelson, Inc. Used by permission. All rights reserved.

Paperback ISBN-13: 978-1-66289-799-3
Hardcover ISBN-13: 978-1-66289-800-6
eBook ISBN-13: 978-1-66289-801-3

ACKNOWLEDGEMENTS

I give all the glory to God my Creator and Heavenly Father, my Lord and Savior Jesus Christ and The Holy Spirit. I thank God for entrusting me with His gifts and I'm grateful to be His daughter; serving Him is my main priority.

I honor and love my beloved parents, John and Henrietta Freeman, who have transitioned from this life and are present with The Lord; they embedded the Word of God and the principles of life in me.

The Freeman Family (my brothers and sisters) are phenomenal, and I'm sincerely thankful for their support.

Special thanks to my mentor and friend, Minister J.L.P; I appreciate your prayers.

DEDICATION

I want to dedicate this book to my sisters who work in education. I admire the example you've set in being committed to helping children excel to their highest potential. I also want to dedicate this book to children all over the world and let them know that Jesus loves them, and they are destined for greatness.

TABLE OF CONTENTS

Acknowledgements.................................v
Dedication......................................vii
Introduction xi

My Prayer For You 1
Faith-Based Affirmations Work By Faith
    and Confessing...............................3
My Personal Experience 13
What Can Faith-Based Affirmations Do?...........21
Who Should Recite Affirmations?.................23
Testimonials....................................33
Faith-Based Affirmations With Scriptures
    For Children.................................37
Seven (7) Prayers For Your Children..............51
    Image.......................................51
    Obedience...................................51
    The Blessing................................ 52
    Divine Protection...........................53
    Intelligence 54

The Anointing of Faith-Based Affirmations

    Soundness of Mind 55
    The Anointing................................ 56

Closing Prayer................................... 57
Glossary 59
References 61

INTRODUCTION

(FAITH-BASED AFFIRMATIONS)

I was inspired to write this book by The Holy Spirit to share my experience with parents about the power of using faith-based affirmations with their children. **What is an affirmation?** The act of affirming or asserting as true; opposed to negation or denial: That which is asserted; position declared as true. (**Webster's Dictionary 1828**) **What is affirm?** To assert positively; to tell with confidence; to aver; to declare the existence of something; to maintain as true; opposed to deny. (**Webster's Dictionary 1828**) Affirmations can be confessing positive words of life, declarations, and proclamations. For several years I worked as a special education teaching assistant. I've always had a passion for teaching children, and I come from a family of educators. Four of my sisters hold post graduate degrees in education. During my time as a special education teaching assistant, The Lord gave me a solution to implement positive affirmations daily to motivate and encourage students; this would also provide academic, behavior and functional improvement.

God loves children and He has an awesome plan for their life. **Psalms 127:3 (nkjv)** – *Behold, children are a heritage from the Lord, The fruit of the womb is a reward.* Children are a blessing and God's plan is that your child prospers in every area of life. **3 John 1:2 (ampc)** – *Beloved, I pray that you may prosper in every way and [that your body] may keep well, even as [I know] your soul keeps well and prospers.* **Psalms 115:14 (nkjv)** – *May the Lord give you increase more and more, You and your children.* The enemy seeks to distort the image of children by planting seeds of low self-esteem. **John 10:10 (ampc)** – *The thief comes only in order to steal and kill and destroy. I came that they may have and enjoy life, and have it in abundance (to the full, till it [a] overflows).* Jesus loves your children, and He came that they might have life and enjoy it abundantly. It is common that some school age children face peer pressure, and they might struggle with their image, identity, self-worth and acceptance. **Matthew 19:14** *(ampc)* – *But He said, Leave the children alone! Allow the little ones to come to Me, and do not forbid or restrain or hinder them, for of such [as these] is the kingdom of heaven composed.* As a parent you have authority to speak life and The Word of God over your children through faith-based affirmations.

> **Ephesians 6:4 (ampc)** – *Fathers, do not irritate and provoke your children to anger [do not exasperate them to resentment], but rear them*

[tenderly] in the training and discipline and the counsel and admonition of the Lord.

Faith-based affirmations use scriptures from The Holy Bible to speak God's promises over your child by faith. There is power in your words and what you speak out of your mouth. **Proverbs 18:21 (ampc)** – *Death and life are in the power of the tongue, and they who indulge in it shall eat the fruit of it [for death or life].* Affirmations will provide for your child; confidence building, refine their image, give them security, stability, and structure. You must have faith when you speak life and The Word of God over your child. Children need to be validated and to know that they are loved, accepted and important. When using faith-based affirmations, it requires these eight key components: prayer, faith, consistency, patience, wisdom, the right posture, commitment, and most importantly love. As a parent you will break barriers when you communicate with love. A child that receives love can be reached on many levels. Love is a powerful force that God created for us to embrace. Love sacrifices and it gives. Love cancels fear and timidity. Love can change the way a person thinks, feels, and responds.

John 3:16 (ampc) – *For God so greatly loved and dearly prized the world that He [even] gave up His only begotten ([a]unique) Son, so that whoever* *believes in (trusts in, clings to, relies on) Him shall not perish (come to destruction, be lost) but have eternal (everlasting) life.*

1 John 4:18 (ampc) – *There is no fear in love [dread does not exist], but full-grown (complete, perfect) love [a]turns fear out of doors and expels every trace of terror! For fear [b]brings with it the thought of punishment, and [so] he who is afraid has not reached the full maturity of love [is not yet grown into love's complete perfection].*

1 John 4:8 (nkjv) – *He who does not love does not know God, for God is love.*

1 Corinthians 13:8 (nkjv) – *"Love never fails."*

MY PRAYER FOR YOU

I pray that as parents are reading this book that The God of our Lord Jesus Christ, The Father of glory, may give unto you the spirit of wisdom and revelation in the knowledge of Him and that the eyes of your understanding would be enlightened, that you may know what is the hope of His calling by confirming The Word of God over your children by faith and that their lives are transformed in Jesus Name! Amen!

FAITH-BASED AFFIRMATIONS WORK BY FAITH AND CONFESSING

What is faith? *Now faith is the assurance (the confirmation, the title deed) of the things we hope for, being the proof of things we do not see and the conviction of their reality [faith perceiving as real fact what is not revealed to the senses].* **Hebrews 11:1 (ampc)**

What is confessing? Owning; avowing; declaring to be true or real; granting or admitting by assent. (**Webster's Dictionary 1828**)

> **Mark 11:22-24 (nkjv)** – *So Jesus answered and said to them, "Have faith in God. For assuredly, I say to you, whoever says to this mountain, 'Be removed and be cast into the sea,' and does not doubt in his heart, but believes that those things he says will be done, he will have whatever he says. Therefore I say to you, whatever things you ask when you pray, believe that you receive them, and you will have them.*

The reason why faith and confessing are important for the faith-based affirmations to work is because your heart, mind and words must be in agreement to see the manifestation of it.

> **Romans 10:10 (ampc)** – *For with the heart a person believes (adheres to, trusts in, and relies on Christ) and so is justified (declared righteous, acceptable to God), and with the mouth he confesses (declares openly and speaks out freely his faith) and confirms [his] salvation.*

Faith is a spiritual force, and it must be developed. What you believe comes out of your heart (spirit) which is where faith is developed. Whatever is in your heart, will come out of your mouth. You develop your faith by meditating what God says in His Word and then start confessing it out of your mouth every day. Also opposition will arise to discourage you from speaking what you desire. You must never focus on what you see in the natural, because what you see in the natural is a temporal state. The enemy will magnify things to make them appear far worse than what they really are. Words are powerful, because they are spirit and life. **John 6:63 (ampc)** – *It is the Spirit Who gives life [He is the Life-giver]; the flesh conveys no benefit whatever [there is no profit in it]. The words (truths) that I have been speaking to* *you are spirit and life.* You have the power and authority to speak life, death, good, bad, blessing or cursing out of your mouth. **Proverbs 18:21 (ampc)** – *Death and life are in the power of the tongue, and they who indulge in it shall eat the fruit of it [for death or life].* When you say something continually, it'll develop faith in your spirit. As you speak by faith believing in your heart with no doubt, you'll see the manifestation of it. Whether you speak positively or negatively, it'll produce what you speak.

> **Deuteronomy 30:19 (nkjv)** – *I call heaven and earth as witnesses today against you, that I have set before you life and death, blessing and cursing; therefore choose life, that both you and your descendants may live;*

For example, if your child is having a hard time remembering things or where they put something. I suggest that you not speak negative to them by saying "You're so forgetful and you can't remember anything". If you do this, you can affect how your child feels about themselves. They'll start to believe that they are forgetful, because you spoke it over them, and they'll start confessing the same thing. **Matthew 12:37 (nkjv)** – *For by your words you will be justified, and by your words you will be condemned."* Reverse those words and start confessing The Word of God over your child according to **Proverbs 10:7 (nkjv)** – *"The memory of the righteous is blessed"*. Parent speak this; (Child's Name) your memory is righteous, blessed and you have excellent recall. Then have your child say "My memory is righteous, blessed and I have excellent recall. When you're speaking life over your child through The Word of God, it'll develop faith in their heart to believe what's being spoken.

If you have spoken negative words over your child, it may take some time to see new results, because words are seeds and they will produce what you speak. Patience is a requirement. Those old seeds must be removed, and new seeds must be planted. **Matthew 15:13 (ampc)** – *He answered, Every plant which My heavenly Father has not planted will be torn up by the roots.* **How do you remove old seeds?** 1st you remove old seeds by repenting and asking God to forgive you of every negative word you spoke about your child. **What is repentance?** Repentance is a change of mind, or a conversion from sin to God; Sorrow for anything done or said; the pain or grief which a person experiences in consequence of the injury or inconvenience produced by his own conduct. **(Webster's Dictionary 1828) 1 John 1:9** – *If we [freely] admit that we have sinned and confess our sins, He is faithful and just (true to His own nature and promises) and will forgive our sins [dismiss our lawlessness] and [continuously] cleanse us from all unrighteousness [everything not* *in conformity to His will in purpose, thought, and action].* Then you can start planting new seeds and confessing what God says about your child. **Luke 8:11 (ampc)** – *"The seed is the Word of God".* We must put the right seed (words) in our heart and speak them by faith. The Word of God is seed, which is what God has given to us because He loves us. It's the same with your child, when you speak life over your child through The Word of God, you're showing them love which will cause them to feel loved, accepted, and important. This will give them security, stability and structure.

These are eight (8) key components required to see results:

- **Pray** – Bring your desire before The Lord concerning your child and ask Him to help you, give you understanding and strengthen you. **Hebrews 4:16 (nkjv)** – *Let us therefore come boldly to the throne of grace, that we may obtain mercy and find grace to help in time of need.*
- **Walk in love** – Love represents selflessness, putting someone else's needs before your own. Love gives. Love isn't afraid or timid. Show gentleness and compassion. **1 Corinthians 13:8 (nkjv)** – *"Love never fails."*

- **Exercise faith** – Believe in your heart that what you see in the natural can change supernaturally by saying what you desire out of your mouth. Keep saying it faithfully until you see the manifestation. **James 2:17 (ampc)** – *So also faith, if it does not have works (deeds and actions of obedience to back it up), by itself is destitute of power (inoperative, dead).*
- **Stay consistent** – Don't waver in what you're confessing. Stand your ground in speaking life and maintain a position of victory. Be constant with your actions of reciting the affirmations daily. **James 1:8 (ampc)** – *[For being as he is] a man of two minds (hesitating, dubious, irresolute), [he is] unstable and unreliable and uncertain about everything [he thinks, feels, decides].*
- **Have patience** – Patience is developed by embracing the process through trusting God and what He said in His Word. Exemplify temperance. Don't give up or quit! **Psalms 138:2 (nkjv)** – *"For You have magnified Your word above all Your name."*
- **Commitment** – Diligence, dedication and resilience will produce strength. Keep the promise in view, because what you speak, you can have it, if you believe it. **Romans 4:20-21 (ampc)** – *No unbelief or distrust made him waver (doubtingly question) concerning the promise of God, but he grew strong and was empowered*

by faith as he gave praise and glory to God, Fully satisfied and assured that God was able and mighty to keep His word and to do what He had promised.

- **Wisdom** – Knowing what to do, how to do it, when to do it and what to say. Ask God for wisdom. **James 1:5 (nkjv)** – *If any of you lacks wisdom, let him ask of God, who gives to all liberally and without reproach, and it will be given to him.*
- **Posture** – Make eye contact with your children and talk to them as a person who understands. When you talk to your child on their level making eye contact and speak directly to them; you will establish a level of trust and comfort creating a non-threatening position which enables you to reach them. **Ephesians 6:4 (nkjv)** – *A soft answer turns away wrath, But a harsh word stirs up anger.*

Hebrews 6:12 (ampc) – *In order that you may not grow disinterested and become [spiritual] sluggards, but imitators, behaving as do those who through faith ([a]by their leaning of the entire personality on God in Christ in absolute trust and confidence in His power, wisdom, and goodness) and by practice of patient endurance and waiting are [now] inheriting the promises.*

Hebrews 4:12-13 (ampc) – *For the Word that God speaks is alive and full of power [making it active, operative, energizing, and effective]; it is sharper than any two-edged sword, penetrating to the dividing line of the [a]breath of life (soul) and [the immortal] spirit, and of joints and marrow [of the deepest parts of our nature], exposing and sifting and analyzing and judging the very thoughts and purposes of the heart. And not a creature exists that is concealed from His sight, but all things are open and exposed, naked and defenseless to the eyes of Him with Whom we have to do.*

This is the power of faith-based affirmations through speaking The Word of God over your child and them speaking The Word of God over themselves.

Faith is the main activator!!! You must believe that what you say is what your child can become or is becoming. If you believe it, your child will also believe it about themselves. The anointing is the power of God active. Activation is to set something in motion by speaking it forth.

MY PERSONAL EXPERIENCE

For several years as a one-on-one special education teaching assistant, I supported students with an individual education plan (IEP) and diverse disabilities. I've always believed in my heart that children with varying disabilities have the potential to excel in education. I was assigned a student that had an (IEP) and who was in a special education classroom. My assignment was to support and help in meeting the academic, behavioral, and functional goals of the student.

This young scholar was five years old and was extremely intelligent, gifted, brilliant and had a loving personality that made you smile. I made observations and noticed that the student had difficulty sitting for extended periods of time, and focusing, and had some behavioral challenges. As a teacher, I discovered that for me to reach this student, I had to develop a connection with them through communicating with love. A child can sense when you genuinely care for them and when you don't.

Some people might be afraid to work with children with varying disabilities, because of the support that may be required. It can be exhausting physically, mentally, and emotionally depending on the needs of that student. When you're working in this field, you must be compassionate, full of love, and have patience, and more.

I prayed and asked God to show me how to help this student. The Lord told me to write out positive affirmations and recite them every day with the student in the morning at school before class. **Matthew 21:22 (ampc)** – *And whatever you ask for in prayer, having faith and [really] believing, you will receive.* As a result of me sincerely praying in faith and asking God for help, He gave me the answer and solution. I started immediately with the affirmations. This is a sample affirmation list of what I wrote: I am smart, I am intelligent, I am loved, I am important, I exercise self-control, I am a great listener, I work well with others, I follow directions, I have excellent recall, I focus in class and I am an excellent student.

This was something new for the student, and it took some time for them to become acclimated to reciting the affirmations every day. However, I had to be consistent in creating a system of structure that would help set the tone for their day and to instill in them that they were capable of learning. I noticed that the student's behavior started to change within several weeks and I saw improvement. As I would speak the affirmations to the student and had them to follow; it began to transform them and the change was noticeable amongst my peers. Speaking positive words of life gave the student confidence, reassurance, security, stability and structure. The student began to focus more, sit for extended periods of time, participate in class, follow directions, complete their assignments; and were able to engage in learning with other students becoming socially acclimated. In less than six months after I started working with the student improvement was made. Their progress was immense and evident.

The young scholar was transferred from a special education classroom to a regular general education classroom. This was a major accomplishment and I give all the glory to God. My heart rejoiced seeing this young scholar excel in school. I supported this student from age five to eight years old; that remained in a general education classroom. I attribute the progress of the student to also using the eight key components.

I did experience some challenges, but I was determined to help this student by; praying, walking in love, exercising faith, being consistent, having patience, staying committed, applying wisdom, and maintaining the right posture. There were many times I became mentally, emotionally and physically exhausted and overwhelmed because I wasn't seeing the results as quickly as I wanted to. However, I learned that I had to trust the process and rely on my faith in God who gave me the formula and that I wasn't doing this in my own strength.

> **Mark 4:28-29 (ampc)** – *The earth produces [acting] by itself—first the blade, then the ear, then the full grain in the ear. But when the grain is ripe and permits, immediately he [a]sends forth [the reapers] and puts in the sickle, because the harvest stands ready.*

For example: If you plant a flower seed in the ground, there is a process for that seed to develop, produce and be transformed into a beautiful flower. A flower seed needs to be nurtured; it must be watered, cultivated, and receive sunlight. These affirmations were seeds of words designed to create change in the life of this student. Using the eight key components was part of the cultivation and nurturing process; which caused a transformation to happen. **Genesis 8:22 (nkjv)** – *While the earth remains, seedtime and harvest, cold and heat, summer and winter, and day and night shall not cease.* Plant the seed, nurture the seed and you will see the manifestation of it. You must see the end result from the beginning. Having a vision and picture will encourage you to stay the course. Receiving this revelation that it was God in me that was doing the work was enlightening and gave me an inner peace.

> **John 14:10 (ampc)** – *Do you not believe that I am in the Father, and that the Father is in Me? What I am telling you I do not say on My own authority and of My own accord; but the Father Who lives continually in Me does the ([a]His) works (His own miracles, deeds of power).*

I was given an additional assignment to support another student that was in a general education classroom. My assignment was to help in meeting the academic, behavioral and functional goals of the student. This young scholar was five years old and extremely intelligent, smart and bright with a loving personality. I used the same formula and recited positive affirmations every day along with the eight key components. The student made progress immediately and began to improve; they were able to focus, follow directions, complete their assignments, sit for extended periods of time, participate in class and engage in learning with the other students becoming socially acclimated. I had a split schedule of working with a first grader and third grader both with IEP's for four months. My days were lengthy, and I was grateful for the support of the staff who encouraged me.

Occasionally, the students would demonstrate emotional frustration. Change can be uncomfortable and cause a negative reaction. I had to be mindful of their needs, sensitive, show empathy and communicate the importance of emotions being a part of a human expression. However, I stayed consistent. I used a redirection method of reminding the students of their affirmations, which would set them back on track. I would also incorporate breaks throughout the day, allow them to play a fun activity or take a walk so they could remain balanced, recharge, and refresh to have a successful school day. It's also important to have incentives and rewards.

Children need to receive your support, approval and validation. I taught students that rewards must be earned, and it was also a motivator. For example: when I would get good grades at school, my parents would reward me. The students began to embrace the affirmations and would be excited to recite them every day. They became acclimated and were able to recall their affirmations. They started to believe what they were saying. Faith was being developed in their heart and spirit; and they were becoming what they were speaking. There is power in the spoken word and coming in agreement with another.

Rehearsing a particular thing repeatedly will produce the fruit of it. It brought me so much joy to help in meeting the academic, behavioral, and functional goals of the students. I loved seeing these young scholars excel in school. I give all the glory to God!

WHAT CAN FAITH-BASED AFFIRMATIONS DO?

- Transform an individual's life through the power of the spoken word
- Build confidence and refine one's image
- Raise one's self-esteem
- Bring security and structure
- Bring mental/emotional clarity and stability
- Eliminate fear and anxiety
- Produce faith
- Develop social skills
- Reset and restructure the behavior of your child
- Put your child in a better position to learn and soar academically
- Manage your child's behaviors
- Help your child improve academically, emotionally and socially

Job 22:28 (ampc) – *You will also declare a thing, And it will be established for you; So light will shine on your ways.*

WHO SHOULD RECITE AFFIRMATIONS?

Both the parent and the child should recite the affirmations every day.

At what age should your child begin their affirmations? Parents, as soon as your child can talk and repeat words and phrases after you, they should start. I believe the younger they are, the more effective results you will see as they grow and develop. Children absorb a lot of information at an early age and their brains are like sponges; they are able retain what they see, hear and have been taught. I've seen small children between the ages of three, four and five that memorized lyrics to songs. Some children learn by audio (hearing), visual (seeing) or both. So, if a child can memorize a song, they can learn and memorize affirmations.

Parents you have influence over your children and you're the foundation layers. You must lead by example. You're the first teacher and it's your responsibility.

> **Proverbs 22:6 (ampc)** – *Train up a child in the way he should go [and in keeping with his individual gift or bent], and when he is old he will not depart from it.*

For example:

Parent: <u>Child's Name</u>, you are smart, bold, important, respectful and patient

Child: I am smart, bold, important, respectful and patient

There is power in agreement.

Agreement – Concord; harmony; conformity. Union of minds in regard to a transfer of interest. (**Webster's Dictionary 1828**)

You as the parent are creating a unified cord of agreement with your child by saying the affirmations with them. Parents, I encourage you to speak the affirmations over your child, then have them repeat after you. This will build confidence in your child, giving them security, stability and structure.

> **2 Cor. 13:1(nkjv)** – *This will be the third time I am coming to you. "By the mouth of two or three witnesses every word shall be established."*

This scripture tells you the power of two coming together speaking forth a matter and then it will be settled.

I encourage you to write out the faith-based affirmations. Having a visual will create a mental picture for the child and they'll begin to see themselves in that manner.

> **Hab. 2:2-3 (nkjv)** – *"Write the vision And make it plain on tablets, That he may run who reads it. For the vision is yet for an appointed time; But at the end it will speak, and it will not lie. Though it tarries, wait for it; Because it will surely come, It will not tarry.*

As you read them aloud, you're releasing faith in the atmosphere of what you desire, which is in alignment with The Word of God. When you say them aloud it will shift things in the atmosphere setting it in motion so that it can come into existence. It will also build your faith and confidence in what you're saying.

Remember to refer to the eight (8) key components that are required to see results:

- **Pray** – Bring your desire before The Lord concerning your child and ask Him to help you, give you understanding and strengthen you. **Hebrews 4:16 (nkjv)** – *Let us therefore come boldly to the throne*

The Anointing of Faith-Based Affirmations

of grace, that we may obtain mercy and find grace to help in time of need.

- **Walk in love** – Love represents selflessness, putting someone else's needs before your own. Love gives. Love isn't afraid or timid. Show gentleness and compassion. **1 Corinthians 13:8 (nkjv)** – *"Love never fails."*

- **Exercise faith** – Believe in your heart that what you see in the natural can change supernaturally by saying what you desire out of your mouth. Keep saying it faithfully until you see the manifestation. **James 2:17 (ampc)** – *So also faith, if it does not have works (deeds and actions of obedience to back it up), by itself is destitute of power (inoperative, dead).*

- **Stay consistent** – Don't waver in what you're confessing. Stand your ground in speaking life and maintain a position of victory. Be constant with your actions of reciting the affirmations daily. **James 1:8 (ampc)** – *[For being as he is] a man of two minds (hesitating, dubious, irresolute), [he is] unstable and unreliable and uncertain about everything [he thinks, feels, decides].*

- **Have patience** – Patience is developed by embracing the process through trusting God and what He said in His Word. Exemplify temperance. Don't give up or quit! **Psalms 138:2 (nkjv)** – *"For You have magnified Your word above all Your name."*

- **Commitment** – Diligence, dedication and resilience will produce strength. Keep the promise in view, because what you speak, you can have it, if you believe it. **Romans 4:20-21 (ampc)** – *No unbelief or distrust made him waver (doubtingly question) concerning the promise of God, but he grew strong and was empowered by faith as he gave praise and glory to God, Fully satisfied and assured that God was able and mighty to keep His word and to do what He had promised.*
- **Wisdom** – Knowing what to do, how to do it, when to do it and what to say. Ask God for wisdom. **James 1:5 (nkjv)** – *If any of you lacks wisdom, let him ask of God, who gives to all liberally and without reproach, and it will be given to him.*
- **Posture** – Make eye contact with your children and talk to them as a person who understands. When you talk to your child on their level making eye contact and speak directly to them; you will establish a level of trust and comfort creating a non-threatening position which enables you to reach them. **Ephesians 6:4 (nkjv)** – *A soft answer turns away wrath, But a harsh word stirs up anger.*

Say them from your heart. When you speak out of your mouth, what you believe in your heart, you'll see the manifestation of it. Your heart and mind must be in agreement to see the manifestation of the affirmations.

Proverbs 23:7 (ampc) – *"For as he thinks in his heart, so is he."*

Romans 10:10 (ampc) – *For with the heart a person believes (adheres to, trusts in, and relies on Christ) and so is justified (declared righteous, acceptable to God), and with the mouth he confesses (declares openly and speaks out freely his faith) and confirms [his] salvation.*

Hebrews 4:14 (ampc) – *Inasmuch then as we have a great High Priest Who has [already] ascended and passed through the heavens, Jesus the Son of God, let us hold fast our confession [of faith in Him].*

Who Should Recite Affirmations?

Me and my beloved parents.

The Anointing of Faith-Based Affirmations

My Father and Mother. I love my parents!

I was 2 years old standing in the pulpit at church. My mother said that I would preach when I grew up. Decades later, in June of 2023, I graduated from ministry school. I'm a minister of the gospel of Jesus Christ. The words that my mother spoke over my life came to fruition and manifested. My Father also released a blessing over my life that is continuously manifesting. I came in agreement with my parents as I would hear it.

The Anointing of Faith-Based Affirmations

TESTIMONIALS

(IN ORDER TO PROTECT THE PRIVACY OF THESE INDIVIDUALS, THEIR NAMES ARE NOT MENTIONED; THESE STATEMENTS ARE TRUE AND WERE MADE BY FORMER CO-WORKERS TO THE AUTHOR, FLORINE G. FREEMAN)

Ms. Freeman constantly and consistently is a calming presence to anyone she encounters, especially the students that she works with. The work and presence that she makes on a first grader that struggles with functioning in a general classroom setting is nothing short of a wonder. She starts the day off with positive affirmations, assuring that the student knows that they are smart, confident, and capable. She also has a way of making adults around her comfortable and cared for as well. She is a constant source of encouragement and a fountain of wisdom. – Year 2022

It is her dedication, her constant ability to empower students in every encounter, and her commitment to her students that make her the excellent teacher that she is. Ms. Freeman encourages students to do their best by instilling an unwavering belief in them and their power. Each and every day, Ms. Freeman greets her students with affirmations made specifically for them to read and repeat to remind them of who they are and who they can be that day. Ms. Freeman is not only an advocate for her students but is often a support to the teachers she works with as well. – Year 2022

When I think of Ms. Freeman, I think of wisdom. She has a deep knowledge and understanding of each student she works with. When I think of Ms. Freeman, I think of enthusiasm and encouragement. Ms. Freeman believes in each student and challenges them to be the best they can be. She is their own personal cheerleader. When I think of Ms. Freeman, I think of dedication. She is dedicated to making sure that each student feels loved. – Year 2022

There was never a day that I would walk through the hallway and not see Ms. Freeman supporting a student in reciting positive affirmations with a student she worked with that were applied all day as behavioral support. Ms. Freeman is kind, compassionate and patient with those who are struggling with their class work. She works with them one-on-one to keep them from falling behind. Even if she was assigned to one student, she helped all students in need without ever being requested. Ms. Freeman has the ability to see the full picture in all situations to ensure effectiveness throughout the day. – Year 2022

Ms. Freeman worked with students who struggled in certain areas in small groups to help them understand the lesson being taught. This was a tough year with many emotions and Ms. Freeman stayed positive and encouraged the students daily with affirmations. – Year 2021

FAITH-BASED AFFIRMATIONS WITH SCRIPTURES FOR CHILDREN

Isaiah 54:13 (nkjv) – *All your children shall be taught by the LORD, And great shall be the peace of your children.*

Parent: You speak the affirmations over your child first

Child: Have your child repeat the affirmations after you

The Anointing of Faith-Based Affirmations

If your child is struggling with a poor self-image and loving themselves and others; speak this:

- I AM MADE IN THE IMAGE OF GOD
- I AM FEARFULLY AND WONDERFULLY MADE
- GOD LOVES ME
- JESUS LOVES ME
- I AM LOVED
- I AM AMAZING
- I LOVE MYSELF AND I LOVE OTHERS

Scripture ref.

Genesis 1:27 (nkjv) — So God created man in His *own* image; in the image of God He created him; male and female He created them.

Psalms 139:14 (nkjv) — I will praise You, for [a]I am fearfully *and* wonderfully made; Marvelous are Your works, And *that* my soul knows very well.

1 John 4:11 (nkjv) — Beloved, if God so loved us, we also ought to love one another.

Galatians 2:20 (nkjv) — I have been crucified with Christ; it is no longer I who live, but Christ lives in me; and the *life* which I now live in the flesh I live by faith in the Son of God, who loved me and gave Himself for me.

Matthew 22:39 (ampc) — And a second is like it: You shall love your neighbor as [you do] yourself.

John 3:16 (ampc) — For God so greatly loved *and* dearly prized the world that He [even] gave up His only begotten ([a]unique) Son, so that whoever believes in (trusts in, clings to, relies on) Him shall not perish (come to destruction, be lost) but have eternal (everlasting) life.

If your child is struggling with fear; speak this:

- I HAVE NO FEAR
- I AM BOLD
- I HAVE THE MIND OF CHRIST JESUS
- I HAVE A SOUND MIND
- I HAVE ANGELS PROTECTING ME

Scripture ref.

2 Timothy 1:7 (ampc) — For God did not give us a spirit of timidity (of cowardice, of craven and cringing and fawning fear), but [He has given us a spirit] of power and of love and of calm *and* well-balanced mind *and* discipline *and* self-control.

Proverbs 28:1 (nkjv) — "But the righteous are bold as a lion."

Philippians 2:5 (nkjv) — Let this mind be in you which was also in Christ Jesus,

Psalms 91:11 (ampc) — For He will give His angels [especial] charge over you to accompany *and* defend *and* preserve you in all your ways [of obedience and service].

If your child is struggling with confidence and low self-esteem; speak this:

- I HAVE CONFIDENCE
- I AM A LEADER
- I AM COURAGEOUS
- I AM A PROBLEM-SOLVER,
- I AM AT THE TOP OF MY CLASS

Scripture ref.

Deuteronomy 28:13 (ampc) — And the Lord shall make you the head, and not the tail; and you shall be above only, and you shall not be beneath, if you heed the commandments of the Lord your God which I command you this day and are watchful to do them. And the Lord shall make you the head, and not the tail; and you shall be above only, and you shall not be beneath, if you heed the commandments of the Lord your God which I command you this day and are watchful to do them.

Psams 23:4 (ampc) — Yes, though I walk through the [deep, sunless] valley of the shadow of death, I will fear *or* dread no evil, for You are with me; Your rod [to protect] and Your staff [to guide], they comfort me.

Isaiah 41:10 (ampc) — Fear not [there is nothing to fear], for I am with you; do not look around you in terror *and* be dismayed, for I am your God. I will strengthen *and* harden you to difficulties, yes, I will help you; yes, I will hold you up *and* retain you with My [victorious] right hand of rightness *and* justice.

Deuteronomy 31:6 (ampc) — Be strong, courageous, *and* firm; fear not nor be in terror before them, for it is the Lord your God Who goes with you; He will not fail you or forsake you.

If your child is struggling academically with grades and comprehension; speak this:

- I AM SMART
- I AM INTELLIGENT
- I RECEIVE KNOWLEDGE
- I RECEIVE EXCELLENT GRADES,
- I RECEIVE UNDERSTANDING
- I RECEIVE WISDOM AND I EXCEL ACADEMICALLY
- I FOCUS AND I COMPLETE ALL MY ASSIGNMENTS

Scripture ref.

Isaiah 11:2 (ampc) — And the Spirit of the Lord shall rest upon Him—the Spirit of wisdom and understanding, the Spirit of counsel and might, the Spirit of knowledge and of the reverential *and* obedient fear of the Lord—

Proverbs 2:6 (ampc) — For the Lord gives skillful *and* godly Wisdom; from His mouth come knowledge and understanding.

Proverbs 18:15 (ampc) — The mind of the prudent is ever getting knowledge, and the ear of the wise is ever seeking (inquiring for and craving) knowledge.

If your child is struggling with showing respect and following instructions; speak this:

- I AM OBEDIENT TO MY PARENTS AND ELDERS
- I AM RESPECTFUL
- I RESPECT MYSELF AND OTHERS
- I RECEIVE INSTRUCTIONS
- I AM A GREAT LISTENER

Scripture ref.

Ephesians 6:1-3 (nkjv) — Children, obey your parents in the Lord, for this is right. ² "Honor your father and mother," which is the first commandment with promise: ³ "that it may be well with you and you may live long on the earth."

Proverbs 1:8 (ampc) — My son, hear the instruction of your father; reject not *nor* forsake the teaching of your mother.

Hebrews 13:17 (nkjv) — Obey those who [a]rule over you, and be submissive, for they watch out for your souls, as those who must give account. Let them do so with joy and not with grief, for that would be unprofitable for you.

Proverbs 8:33 (ampc) — Hear instruction and be wise, and do not refuse *or* neglect it.

If your child is struggling with remembering things or with clarity; speak this:

- MY MEMORY IS RIGHTEOUS AND BLESSED
- I HAVE EXCELLENT RECALL
- I HAVE CLARITY OF THOUGHT
- I SPEAK WITH CLARITY AND UNDERSTANDING

Scripture ref.

Proverbs 10:7 (nkjv) – "The memory of the righteous *is* blessed,"

John 14:26 (ampc) — But the Comforter (Counselor, Helper, Intercessor, Advocate, Strengthener, Standby), the Holy Spirit, Whom the Father will send in My name [in My place, to represent Me and act on My behalf], He will teach you all things. And He will cause you to recall (will remind you of, bring to your remembrance) everything I have told you.

John 16:13 (nkjv) — However, when He, the Spirit of truth, has come, He will guide you into all truth; for He will not speak on His own *authority*, but whatever He hears He will speak; and He will tell you things to come.

The Anointing of Faith-Based Affirmations

If your child is struggling with being kind and becoming socially acclimated; speak this:

- I AM KIND
- I AM FRIENDLY
- I AM HELPFUL
- I HAVE EXCELLENT SPEECH AND GREAT SOCIAL SKILLS
- I WORK WELL WITH OTHERS

Scripture ref.

Proverbs 18:24 (nkjv) — A man *who has* friends [a]must himself be friendly,
But there is a friend *who* sticks closer than a brother.

Ephesian 4:29 (ampc) — Let no foul *or* polluting language, *nor* evil word *nor* unwholesome *or* worthless talk [ever] come out of your mouth, but only such [speech] as is good *and* beneficial to the spiritual progress of others, as is fitting to the need *and* the occasion, that it may be a blessing *and* give grace (God's favor) to those who hear it.

Colossians 3:12 (nkjv) — Therefore, as *the* elect of God, holy and beloved, put on tender mercies, kindness, humility, meekness, longsuffering;

If your child is struggling with lethargy and lack of energy; speak this:

- I AM HEALTHY
- I AM ENERGETIC AND FULL OF STAMINA
- I WALK IN DIVINE HEALTH
- I SHALL LIVE A LONG FRUITFUL LIFE

Scripture ref.

3 John 1:2 (ampc) — Beloved, I pray that you may prosper in every way and [that your body] may keep well, even as [I know] your soul keeps well *and* prospers.

1 Peter 2:24 (nkjv) — who Himself bore our sins in His own body on the tree, that we, having died to sins, might live for righteousness—by whose [a]stripes you were healed.

Psalms 91:16 (ampc) — With long life will I satisfy him and show him My salvation.

Psalms 103:5 (nkjv) — Who satisfies your mouth with good *things*, *So that* your youth is renewed like the eagle's.

If your child struggles with anger; speak this:

- I AM PEACEFUL
- I AM CALM
- I THINK BEFORE I SPEAK AND ACT

Scripture ref.

Philippians 4:6-7 (nkjv) — Be anxious for nothing, but in everything by prayer and supplication, with thanksgiving, let your requests be made known to God; and the peace of God, which surpasses all understanding, will guard your hearts and minds through Christ Jesus.

Psalms 19:14 (ampc) — Let the words of my mouth and the meditation of my heart be acceptable in Your sight, O Lord, my [firm, impenetrable] Rock and my Redeemer.

Proverbs 4:23-24 (ampc) — Keep *and* guard your heart with all vigilance *and* above all that you guard, for out of it flow the springs of life. Put away from you false *and* dishonest speech, and willful *and* contrary talk put far from you.

If your child is struggling with exercising self-control; speak this:

- I HAVE AN EXCELLENT SPIRIT
- I HAVE SELF-CONTROL
- I EXERCISE SELF-CONTROL
- I AM HONEST AND I SPEAK THE TRUTH
- I AM PATIENT

Scripture ref.

Galatians 5:22-23 (ampc) — But the fruit of the [Holy] Spirit [the work which His presence within accomplishes] is love, joy (gladness), peace, patience (an even temper, forbearance), kindness, goodness (benevolence), faithfulness, Gentleness (meekness, humility), self-control (self-restraint, continence). Against such things there is no law [[a]that can bring a charge].

Proverbs 12:22 (nkjv) — Lying lips *are* an abomination to the LORD, But those who deal truthfully *are* His delight.

John 17:17 (nkjv) — Sanctify[a] them by Your truth. Your word is truth.

Daniel 6:3 (nkjv) — Then this Daniel distinguished himself above the governors and satraps, because an excellent spirit *was* in him; and the king gave thought to setting him over the whole realm.

The Anointing of Faith-Based Affirmations

If your child is struggling with discovering their gifts; speak this:

- I AM GIFTED
- I AM TALENTED
- I AM CREATIVE
- I AM INNOVATIVE

Scripture ref.

Genesis 1:26 (ampc) – "God said, Let Us [Father, Son, and Holy Spirit] make mankind in Our image, after Our likeness,"

Ephesians 2:10 (nkjv) – For we are His workmanship, created in Christ Jesus for good works, which God prepared beforehand that we should walk in them.

James 1:17 (ampc) – Every good gift and every perfect ([a]free, large, full) gift is from above; it comes down from the Father of all [that gives] light, in [the shining of] Whom there can be no variation [rising or setting] or shadow cast by His turning [as in an eclipse].

Proverbs 18:16 (ampc) – A man's gift makes room for him and brings him before great men.

If your child is struggling with future uncertainty; speak this:

- I HAVE A GREAT FUTURE
- I AM BLESSED
- I AM IMPORTANT
- I AM DESTINED FOR GREATNESS
- I HAVE FAVOR WITH GOD AND MAN

Scripture ref.

Jeremiah 29:11 (nkjv) – For I know the thoughts that I think toward you, says the Lord, thoughts of peace and not of evil, to give you a future and a hope.

Numbers 6:24-26 (ampc) – The Lord bless you and watch, guard, *and* keep you; The Lord make His face to shine upon *and* enlighten you and be gracious (kind, merciful, and giving favor) to you; The Lord lift up His [approving] countenance upon you and give you peace (tranquility of heart and life continually).

Isaiah 64:8 (ampc) – Yet, O Lord, You are our Father; we are the clay, and You our Potter, and we all are the work of Your hand. Yet, O Lord, You are our Father; we are the clay, and You our Potter, and we all are the work of Your hand.

Proverbs 3:4-6 (ampc) – So shall you find favor, good understanding, *and* high esteem in the sight [or judgment] of God and man. Lean on, trust in, *and* be confident in the Lord with all your heart *and* mind and do not rely on your own insight *or* understanding. In all your ways know, recognize, *and* acknowledge Him, and He will direct *and* make straight *and* plain your paths.

SEVEN (7) PRAYERS FOR YOUR CHILDREN

Image

Father God in the Name of Jesus, I thank you that my children are made in your image, and they are secure in their God-given identity and gender from birth as a male or female.

Scripture ref.

Genesis 1:27 (nkjv) — So God created man in His *own* image; in the image of God He created him; male and female He created them.

Obedience

Father God in the Name of Jesus, I thank you that my children are a heritage from The Lord as arrows in the hand of a warrior and they are like olive plants round about my table and as they obey and honor their parents, it shall be well with them, and their days shall be long on the earth. I thank you Father that they will obey their elders.

Scripture ref.

Psalms 127:3-4 (nkjv) — Behold, children *are* a heritage from the LORD, The fruit of the womb *is* a reward. Like arrows in the hand of a warrior, So *are* the children of one's youth.

Psalms 128:3 (ampc) – "your children shall be like olive plants round about your table."

Ephesians 6:1-3 (ampc) — Children, obey your parents in the Lord [as His representatives], for this is just and right. Honor (esteem and value as precious) your father and your mother—this is the first commandment with a promise— That all may be well with you and that you may live long on the earth.

The Blessing

Father God in the Name of Jesus, I pray that you bless my children, keep them, make your face to shine upon them, be gracious unto them, Lord lift up your countenance upon them, and give them your peace; bless them indeed enlarge their territory keep your hand upon them and keep them from evil that it may not grieve them or cause them pain.

Seven (7) Prayers For Your Children

Scripture ref.

Numbers 6:24-26 (ampc) — The Lord bless you and watch, guard, *and* keep you; The Lord make His face to shine upon *and* enlighten you and be gracious (kind, merciful, and giving favor) to you; The Lord lift up His [approving] countenance upon you and give you peace (tranquility of heart and life continually).

1 Chronicles 4:10 (nkjv) — And Jabez called on the God of Israel saying, "Oh, that You would bless me indeed, and enlarge my [a] territory, that Your hand would be with me, and that You would keep *me* from evil, that I may not cause pain!" So God granted him what he requested.

Divine Protection

Father God in the Name of Jesus, I thank you that no evil shall befall my children neither shall any plague come near their dwelling for you shall give your angels charge over them to keep them in all of their ways and with long life will you satisfy them and show them your salvation.

Scripture ref.

Psalms 91:10 (nkjv) — No evil shall befall you,
Nor shall any plague come near your dwelling;

Psalms 91:16 (nkjv) — With [a]long life I will satisfy him,
And show him My salvation."

Intelligence

Father God in the Name of Jesus, I thank you that you have made my children ten times better in all matters of wisdom and understanding in all of their realm; because the Spirit of The Lord rest upon them, the Spirit of wisdom and understanding, the Spirit of counsel and might, the Spirit of knowledge and the fear of The Lord. My child's memory is righteous, and it's blessed. For they have supernatural recall, mental and spiritual sharpness, clarity, acuity, keenness, competence, and intelligence.

Scripture ref.

Daniel 1:20 (nkjv) — And in all matters of wisdom *and* understanding about which the king examined them, he found them ten times better than all the magicians *and* astrologers who *were* in all his realm.

Isaiah 11:2 (ampc) — And the Spirit of the Lord shall rest upon Him—the Spirit of wisdom and understanding, the Spirit of counsel and might, the Spirit of knowledge and of the reverential *and* obedient fear of the Lord—

Proverbs 10:7 (nkjv) — "The memory of the righteous *is* blessed,"

Soundness of Mind

Father God in the Name of Jesus, I thank you that my children have the mind of Christ Jesus, and you haven't given them the spirit of fear, but you've given them a spirit of power, love and a sound mind and they think only on the things that are true, noble, just, pure, lovely and are of a good report.

Scripture ref.

Philippians 2:5 (ampc) — Let this same attitude *and* purpose *and* [humble] mind be in you which was in Christ Jesus: [Let Him be your example in humility:]

2 Timothy 1:7 (ampc) — For God did not give us a spirit of timidity (of cowardice, of craven and cringing and fawning fear), but [He has given us a spirit] of power and of love and of calm *and* well-balanced mind *and* discipline *and* self-control.

Philippians 4:8 (nkjv) — Finally, brethren, whatever things are true, whatever things *are* noble, whatever things *are* just, whatever things *are* pure, whatever things *are* lovely, whatever things *are* of good report, if *there is* any virtue and if *there is* anything praiseworthy—meditate on these things.

The Anointing

Father God in the Name of Jesus, I thank you that The Spirit of the Lord is upon my children, because You hath anointed them to preach the gospel to the poor, You hath sent them to heal the brokenhearted, to proclaim liberty to the captives, and recovering of sight to the blind, to set at liberty those who are oppressed, to preach the acceptable year of the Lord.

Scripture ref.

Luke 4:18-19 (nkjv) — "The Spirit of the Lord *is* upon Me, Because He has anointed Me To preach the gospel to *the* poor; He has sent Me [a]to heal the brokenhearted, To proclaim liberty to *the* captives And recovery of sight to *the* blind, *To* set at liberty those who are [b]oppressed; To proclaim the acceptable year of the Lord."

CLOSING PRAYER

Father God in the Name of Jesus, let the words of my mouth and the meditation of my heart be acceptable in thy sight, Oh Lord my strength and my redeemer. I decree that the words that I speak will be full of life reflecting you Lord and thank you for establishing my heart, thoughts and ways as yours in Jesus Name, Amen!

GLOSSARY

Affirm – To assert positively; to tell with confidence; to aver; to declare the existence of something; to maintain as true; opposed to deny.
(Webster's Dictionary 1828)

Affirmation – The act of affirming or asserting as true; opposed to negation or denial: That which is asserted; position declared as true.
(Webster's Dictionary 1828)

Agreement – Concord; harmony; conformity. Union of minds in regard to a transfer of interest.
(Webster's Dictionary 1828))

Confessing – Owning; avowing; declaring to be true or real; granting or admitting by assent.
(Webster's Dictionary 1828)

Consistency – A standing together, as the parts of a system, or of conduct, etc; agreement or harmony of all parts of a complex thing among themselves, or of the

same thing with itself at different times; congruity; uniformity; a state of rest.
(Webster's Dictionary 1828)

Faith – Now faith is the assurance (the confirmation, [a]the title deed) of the things [we] hope for, being the proof of things [we] do not see *and* the conviction of their reality [faith perceiving as real fact what is not revealed to the senses].
(Amplified Bible, Classic Edition)

Patience – Perseverance; constancy in labor or exertion.
(Webster's Dictionary 1828)

Repentance – Repentance is a change of mind, or a conversion from sin to God; Sorrow for anything done or said; the pain or grief which a person experiences in consequence of the injury or inconvenience produced by his own conduct.
(Webster's Dictionary 1828)

REFERENCES

Amplified Bible, Classic Edition (AMPC)

New King James Version (The Holy Bible)

Webster's Dictionary 1828

Printed in the USA
CPSIA information can be obtained
at www.ICGtesting.com
CBHW030808080624
9698CB00001B/118